Shipwrecks of Truk
トラックの沈船

Photographs & Text by Philip Alan Rosenberg

Shipwrecks of Truk

トラックの沈船

Produced by Dr. Grahame Barry, Bill Ryder, & James M. Fey

Edited by Francis X. Hezel, S.J.

Japanese Translation by Etsuo Sekine, S.J.

ISBN-0-9607052-0-1
LCCN-81-90438
© Copyright 1981
by PHILIP ALAN ROSENBERG
All rights reserved
Book design by Philip Alan Rosenberg

Contents

Introduction 7

The Ships 13

The Artifacts 35

The Marine Life 57

The Story 79

Bibliography 102

Introduction

After a half dozen pulls on the starter rope, the battered outboard coughed twice and then roared to life. Mimi, a local Trukese boat driver, reached out for the throttle and slowed the powerful motor down to a hushed murmur. As I released the bow line from the dock, the tidal current edged the small craft away into deeper water. Mimi gunned the throttle and expertly steered us around submerged coral heads that could have pierced the fragile fiberglass hull.

The sky was clear and windless as we sped away from the shallows into open water. The reflection of rich emerald-green islands in the turquoise lagoon was almost too striking to ignore, but I forced myself to concentrate on today's dive.

After eighteen months of exploring and photographing Truk's shipwrecks, this would be my first visit to a wreck discovered only a few weeks earlier. Not more than a handful of divers had seen this ship since her destruction in 1944. Was she a drab pile of wreckage with only a few subtle reminders of her past, or was she a recognizeable transport complete with packed cargo holds, crew's quarters, and bridge? If her superstructure was intact then the chances of finding new artifacts were high; whatever she contained would appear almost unchanged after thirty-seven years. It would be like visiting an undersea museum that had been locked away unseen and untouched, preserved twenty-seven fathoms below the surface of the lagoon. Since my work was to make a photographic survey of the wrecks and their artifacts, this new ship could mean an important addition to the twenty-five already captured on film.

In an effort to preserve the fifty Japanese vessels sunk by U.S. forces in February and April 1944, the Truk District Legislature passed a law designating them an historical monument and prohibiting the removal of any artifacts. Lying at the bottom of Truk's forty mile wide lagoon, these ships contain all the equipment and cargo to be found on any merchant fleet during wartime; under mounds of silt inside dark crew's quarters lay china and glassware, phonograph records, shoes, clothing, books, and numerous other personal effects. Cargo holds contain ship mines, warheads, torpedoes, ammunition, trucks, tanks, fighter planes, land guns, bicycles, bulldozers, beer bottles, and canned food -- supplies necessary for Japan's garrisons in the Pacific.

序

　スターターの紐を5・6回引いて、やっとエンジンがかかった。初め2度ほどブルンブルンとうなり、その後は順調にうなり続けた。トラックで生まれ育ったボートドライバーのミミは、アクセルハンドルを握り、それを緩めた。すると、エンジンの音が軽やかになった。ボートを波止場につないでおくロープをほどくと、潮流がボートの横に打ち当たり、そのボートは、沖の方へと押しやられた。ミミはエンジンを吹かし、馴れた手付きで舵をとった。もし海面下に潜む珊瑚礁に打ち当たりでもすると、グラスファイバーの船体には、すぐ穴があいてしまう。

　空は高く晴れ上がり、風もない。私たちはボートを駆って浅瀬から沖へと乗り出した。真青なラグーンに映るエメラルドグリーンの島影はあまりにも印象的で、人々はその虜になってしまう。しかし私は、強いて今日の潜水に精神を集中した。

　トラックの沈船を一年半も探険し、写真を撮り続けてきたが、今回のは数週間前に発見されたばかりのもので、私も訪れるのは初めてである。昭和19年に沈没してから、この船の姿を見たものは、ほんの一握りに過ぎない。それは昔日の姿をかろうじて留めているガラクタか、それとも、積荷や船室や甲板が完全に残っている貨物船であろうか。もし船の上部構造がもとのままに完全であれば、新しい器物が見つかる公算は大きい。たとえそれがどんなものであろうと、37年後の今もほとんど変化せずにもとの姿を留めているからである。この船に潜ることは、あたかも、ラグーンの海底50メートルに人目にふれず、ひっそりととざされてきた海底博物館を見学するようなものである。私の仕事は、沈船とそこにある器物を写真におさめ調査することであるから、この新たな船は重要な意味をもつ。すでに調査のすんだ25隻の船に、さらに新しいページを加えることになるからである。

　昭和19年の2月と4月に、米軍に沈められた50隻の日本船を保存するために、トラック地区議会は法律を作り、それらを史跡に指定し、器物の移動・除去を禁じた。トラックの60数キロに及ぶラグーンの底に眠っている船には、それが戦時中の商船ならば、今なおあらゆる装備や積荷がそのまま残っている。泥に埋もれたうす暗い乗組員の船室には、陶器、ガラス製品、レコードの音盤、靴、衣類、本、その他数々の手回り品が見い出される。輸送船の船倉には、機雷、弾頭、魚雷、弾薬、トラック、戦車、戦闘機、大砲、自転車、ブルドーザー、ビールびん、缶詰めなどが残っている。それらはみな、南洋に駐屯する日本軍に必要なものであった。　　　　　　　　　　　　　　　　　　しかし、これらの船は、ほとんど忘れ去られようとしている大戦の遺物に過ぎないものではない。それらは長年、浅い、暖かい太平洋の水につかっていたので、今や世界最大の人工珊瑚礁と化し、海洋生活の極美を楽しませてくれている。これらの鋼鉄の船体は残すところなく、色とりどりの造礁珊瑚、ソフトコーラル

But the ships are much more than relics of an almost forgotten war. Years of submersion in the shallow, warm Pacific water have transformed them into one of the world's largest collections of artificial reefs, overgrown with marine life of extraordinary beauty. Every square inch of these steel-hulled vessels is covered with hard and soft corals, sponges, and algae of almost infinite variety and color. The fish life that inhabits these reefs is remarkable -- from thousands of thumbnail-sized transparent opal sweepers to giant twelve-foot long oceanic white-tip sharks and just about every imaginable form of fish life in between. No longer a lifeless testament to the tragedy of war, the shipwrecks of Truk have become magnificent undersea gardens.

This book represents the culmination of my efforts to record images of the sunken fleet. I began photographing exterior and interior views to show how the wrecks have changed after almost four decades of growth and decay. Months later, to symbolize the violence and destruction of the past, I photographed artifacts hidden deep inside crew's quarters and cargo holds. And finally, I photographed the marine life that dwells within these man-made reefs to illustrate the beauty and healing power of the undersea environment.

The result is this book, one that is not the product of my efforts alone. Father Francis X. Hezel, S.J., Director of Micronesian Seminar and Xavier High School in Truk, generously supported my project by providing room and board, airfare, and research material from his history library, in addition to offering advice on the text. Clark and Chineina Graham of Micronesia Aquatics donated all the logistic support so vital for the hundreds of dives that were made for the collection of the photographs. Bill Ryder, an expert diver also of Micronesia Aquatics, graciously spent much of his free time accompanying me on all of the deep decompression dives. His knowledge of the ships was tremendously helpful; without his assistance many of the photographs could not have been made. Scott Russell of the Trust Territory Historic Preservation Office provided funding for all the film and processing necessary for the compiling of photographs for this work. Finally, financial support for the publication of this volume was generously provided by Dr. Grahame Barry, James Fey, and Bill Ryder. I am indebted to these people, for the support and encouragement they so freely gave me.

We cruised south past the northern tip of Dublon Island and entered an area where there are at least ten ships lying 200 feet below on the sandy lagoon floor. When we were seventy-five yards from a shallow, finger-shaped reef, Mimi cut the throttle and our boat slowed to a few knots. He scanned the horizon and found the island coordinates that pinpointed the wreck's location; from the surface there was no indication that there might be a ship below us. Bill dropped the anchor and it quickly disappeared into the lagoon. When the anchor hit bottom he grabbed the thin rope with both hands as Mimi shifted the outboard into reverse. We motored

海綿、藻類に被われている。またこの珊瑚礁に棲息する魚の生活も、実に見事である。親指の爪先大の透明なオパールスイーパーが群れをなして泳ぎ、全長４メートル近くもある巨大な、大洋白鰭鮫も泳いでいる。その間のありとあらゆる大きさの魚が、そこで生活を展開している。トラックの沈船はもはや悲惨な戦争の遺言ではなく、すばらしい海底楽園となっている。

　この本は、海底に沈んだ艦隊の姿を記録しようと努力してきた、その結晶である。沈船がほぼ40年の盛衰を経てどのように変化したかを示すために、まずその外部と内部の景観を写真に撮った。それから数ヶ月して、過去の暴挙と破壊を表現するために、乗組員の船室や船倉に奥深く隠されてきたいろいろな器物の写真もとるようになった。そして最後に、海底生活の美と癒しの力とを示すために、この人工の珊瑚礁に棲息する生物の生活を撮るようになった。

　その結果がこの本である。しかしこれは、私ひとりの力で出来上がったものではない。トラックにあるザビエル高等学校、ミクロネシアセミナーの理事長、フランシス・Ｘ・ヒーゼル神父には、私の企画に賛同していただき、多くの寛大な援助を賜わった。食住から交通費まで、また研究に必要な文献も提供していただき、このテキストを作成するにあたって多くの助言を賜わった。ミクロネシア・アクアティクスの グラハム 夫妻には、数百回にも及ぶ潜水に必要なものをすべて提供していただいた。そのおかげでこの写真ができたのである。また同じミクロネシア・アクアティクスの潜水専門家、ビル・ライダー氏は貴重な時間をさいて、深海に潜る時にはいつも同伴してくださった。彼は船について造詣が深く、その知識は大いに役に立った。もし彼の助けがなければ数多くの写真はとれなかったに違いない。信託統治領史跡保存委員会のスコット・ラッセル氏には、この企画に必要なフィルムと現像料を提供していただいた。最後に、この本の出版のため、グラハム・バリー博士、ジェームズ・フェイ氏、ビル・ライダー氏が、経済的に援助してくださったのである。これらの人々の援助と励ましによって、この本は日の目を見るようになった。ここで、これらの方々の御恩に対して心から感謝の意を表したい。

　さて私たちの乗ったボートは、ドゥブロン（夏島）の北端を過ぎて南に向い、海面下60メートルの砂床に少くとも10隻の船が沈んでいる場所にやってきた。浅瀬にある指状珊瑚礁から80メートルばかり離れた所に来ると、ミミがアクセルを緩め、ボートは減速した。彼は水平線を見回し、沈船のありかを正確に示す島の目印を探した。海面には、下に船が沈んでいるかどうかを示すものは何一つない。ビルが錨を下ろすと、それはみるみるうちにラグーンの中に吸い込まれて行った。錨が底に打ち当たると、ビルはその細いロープを両手で握り、ミミがギアを後進に切り替えた。ボートは近くの珊瑚礁を避け、錨をひきずってゆっくりと進んだ。そして錨が大きな珊瑚にではなく、沈船にひっかかるのを待った。

　突如、ロープはグイッと引っ張られピーンと張った。ビルはそれが確かなものであることを認め、ミミにボートを止めるよう合図した。錨は何か固いものに引っかかり、ちょっとやそっとではびくともしない。それは果して私たちの目指す船であろうか。

ブリッジ内部…富士川丸　　bridge level interior, *Fujikawa Maru*

bow, *Sankisan Maru*　　　船首…山鬼山丸

前部船倉…第二日野丸

forward hold, *Dai na Hino Maru*

bridge superstructure and forward deck, *Shinkoku Maru*　　　　ブリッジ上部構造と前甲板…神国丸

舵機…輸送船（船名不詳）   helm, *Unidentified Transport*

washroom, *Shinkoku Maru*　　　　　　　　　　　　　　　　　　　　浴室…神国丸

操縦室…神国丸　　operating room, *Shinkoku Maru*

port passageway, *Sankisan Maru* 左舷通路…山鬼山丸

湯沸器…桑港丸

water heater and filter, *San Francisco Maru*

galley entrance, *Rio de Janeiro Maru*　　　　　　　　　　炊事場入口…りおで志"やねろ丸

炊事場こんろ…神国丸　　　　　　　　　　　　　　　　　　　galley stove, *Shinkoku Maru*

stern, *Gosei Maru*　　　船尾…五星丸

通信室…清澄丸

communications room, *Kiyosumi Maru*

engine room catwalks, *Unidentified Transport*　　　　機関室の通路…輸送船（船名不詳）

機関室…輸送船（船名不詳）

engine room, *Unidentified Transport*

opal sweepers in hallway, *Fujikawa Maru* 廊下と小魚群（オパールスイーパー）…富士川丸

前方船室…輸送船（船名 不詳） forward cabin, *Unidentified Transport*

bowgun, *Amagisan Maru* 船尾砲…天城山丸

前帆柱…富士川丸

forward mast, *Fujikawa Maru*

The Artifacts
器物

'Zero' fighterplane cockpit, *Fujikawa Maru*　　　零戦の操縦席…富士川丸

4インチ砲弾頭…富士川丸

four-inch warheads, *Fujikawa Maru*

light tank, *San Francisco Maru*　　　　　　　　　　　　　　　　　　　　　　　　　　　小型戦車…桑港丸

薬莢…山鬼山丸

ammunition, *Sankisan Maru*

truck cab interior, *San Francisco Maru*

トラック運転台内部…桑港丸

トラック…桑港丸　　　　　　　　　　　　　　　　　truck, *San Francisco Maru*

ship mines, *San Francisco Maru* 　　　　　　　　　　機雷…桑港丸

機雷…桑港丸　　　　　　　　　　　　　　　　　　　　ship mines, *San Francisco Maru*

bicycles, *Kiyosumi Maru*　　　　　　　　　　　　　　　自転車…清澄丸

道具…輸送船（船名不詳）　　　hand tools, *Unidentified Transport*

gas masks, *Unidentified Transport*

防毒マスク…輸送船（船名不詳）

タイプライター…山霧丸　　typewriter, *Yamagiri Maru*

kerosene bosun's lamps, *Kiyosumi Maru*　　　　石油ランプ…清澄丸

六分儀座…神国丸   sextant, *Shinkoku Maru*

clothing storeroom, *Shinkoku Maru* 衣類倉庫…神国丸

靴…神国丸　　　　　　　　　　　　　　　　　　　　　　shoe, *Shinkoku Maru*

books, *Rio de Janeiro Maru*　　　　本…りおで志゛やねろ丸

鹿の頭蓋骨…輸送船（船名不詳）　　　　　　　　　　　　　　　　deer skull, *Unidentified Transport*

dish cabinet, *Shinkoku Maru*　　　　　　　　　　食器…神国丸

頭蓋骨…神国丸

crewman's skull, *Shinkoku Maru*

The Marine Life
海洋生活

forecastle railing, *Shinkoku Maru*　　　　　　　　　　　　　　　　　　　船首楼の手すり…神国丸

苺珊瑚とオパールスイーパー…神国丸　　strawberry tree coral, *Shinkoku Maru*

engine telegraph and encrusting sponges, *Shinkoku Maru* 操縦管とそれについた海綿…神国丸

オレンジ珊瑚…富士川丸　　orange gorgonian, *Fujikawa Maru*

tree corals on anchor chain, *Sankisan Maru*　　　　錨鎖についた樹状珊瑚…山鬼山丸

中央柱についた指状珊瑚…山鬼山丸　　finger coral on kingpost, *Sankisan Maru*

broccoli coral on deck railing, *Gosei Maru*　　　甲板手すりのブロッコリ珊瑚…五星丸

中央柱についた樹状珊瑚…神国丸   tree coral on kingpost, *Shinkoku Maru*

bridge superstructure and deck railing, *Shinkoku Maru*

ブリッジ上部構造と甲板の手すり…神国丸

戸口と窓…神国丸 doorway and window, *Shinkoku Maru*

baitfish and bridge superstructure, *Shinkoku Maru* 　　小魚群とブリッジ上部構造…神国丸

羅針板…神国丸

bridge compass, *Shinkoku Maru*

strawberry snapper, *Shinkoku Maru*　　　　　　　　　　　　　　　　　　　　　　　　苺鯛…神国丸

舵機とオパールスイーパー…輸送船（船名不詳）　　helm and opal sweepers, *Unidentified Transport*

anchor light, *Sankisan Maru*　　　　　　　　　　　停泊灯…山鬼山丸

運搬機の桁についた管状海綿…富士川丸

pipe sponges on cargo boom, *Fujikawa Maru*

encrusting sponges and fluted oysters on porthole, *Shinkoku Maru*

艙門の海綿と鶏冠牡蠣…神国丸

船体の表面…神国丸

hull surface, *Shinkoku Maru*

encrusting sponges on tank tread, *San Francisco Maru* 　　　　　戦車の車輪についた海綿…桑港丸

闘魚…神国丸

soldier fish, *Shinkoku Maru*

The Story
歴史談

Task Force 58 (National Archives Photo)

第58機動部隊

On February 4, 1944, a Marine PB4Y aircraft flew over Truk Lagoon at 20,000 feet, making the first American photo-reconnaisance of what was then considered Japan's strongest advanced naval anchorage of the Pacific. The photographs revealed the Japanese Combined Fleet under Admiral Koga: one battleship, two carriers, twenty destroyers, ten cruisers, and twelve submarines, along with over fifty merchant vessels.

Warned by this lone American plane that an allied attack was imminent, Admiral Koga ordered all capitol ships to Palau. The large merchant fleet, however, was to remain to unload its desperately needed cargo of fuel, munitions, and food; the Japanese Naval Command was confident that there was still time to supply Truk and escape unharmed. The squadrons of blue Hellcat fighters that appeared over the lagoon early in the morning of February 16 caught Koga's forces totally unprepared and marked the beginning of the end of thirty years of Japanese military domination in the North Pacific.

Truk came under Japanese control in 1914 shortly after the start of World War I. After the Japanese Navy forced the withdrawal of the German fleet stationed in the North Pacific, it seized all German-held islands north of the equator and established military control in the Marshalls, Carolines, Marianas, Yap, and Palau. In doing so, Japan acquired islands that she considered indispensible to the defense of her own coastline, just as America claimed that Hawaii, Midway, Wake, and Guam were essential to safeguard the Pacific coast of the United States. When the islands of Micronesia were transferred from Germany to Japan in 1914 they passed from a nation to which they were of little strategic value to a nation that could use them to great military advantage.

As Germany's defeat in the European war became more certain, Japan moved to legitimize her new Pacific colonies. In 1917, Japan concluded a secret treaty with Great Britain and a handful of other nations assuring her that her claims to Micronesia would be recognized internationally. Finally, at the Versailles Conference of 1922, Japan was formally mandated these islands by the League of Nations and was commissioned to administer their government and internal affairs.

By the mid-1930's dark clouds had once again gathered over the globe. Although forbidden by the terms of the Mandate to build military installations, Japan began its fortification of the islands in earnest. Truk was readied to serve as the advance base of the large, mobile Japanese Navy - - the mightiest in the Pacific at that time.

At the outbreak of the war, Truk was estimated to be the strongest naval base in the Pacific except for Pearl Harbor. It was Truk's natural defenses more than the presence of Japan's Army and Navy that gave it this reputation as an impregnable fortress and as the "Gibralter of the Pacific" A submerged mountain range, Truk's eleven major islands were surrounded by a coral reef 140 miles in circumference. There are only five passes through the outer reef and these could be easily defended by mines and coastal guns. Since no US naval gun had the range to reach any of the military targets from outside the lagoon, any amphibious assault would have to

昭和19年2月4日、米海軍機ＰＢ４Ｙが、トラック環礁2万フィート（約6,100メートル）上空を偵察し、当時太平洋において最強を誇っていた日本海軍基地の写真を初めて入手した。これによって、古賀海軍大将指揮下にある日本艦隊の全容が明らかになった。戦艦1隻、航空母艦2隻、駆逐艦20隻、巡洋艦10隻、潜水艦12隻、それに50隻を越える商船団である。

　この1偵察機から連合軍の攻撃がさし迫っていると見た古賀海将は、すべての主要艦をパラオに移動させた。しかし、商船団は、燃料、弾薬、食料などの必需品の荷下しのために留まらねばならなかった。日本海軍司令部は、トラックへの補給が終ってからでも、余裕をもって、被害を受けずに逃れられるものと確信していた。が、2月16日未明、青い「じゃじゃ馬」戦闘機の中隊が、突如ラグーン上空に現われ、準備体制が全く整っていない古賀連隊を襲撃した。これは北太平洋における30年に及ぶ日本軍支配が終わる幕明けであった。

　トラックは第一次世界大戦開始直後、1914年に、日本の支配下に入った。日本海軍は、北太平洋に配置されていたドイツ艦隊を引き上げさせ、ドイツが統治していた赤道以北の島々を押さえ、マーシャル、カロリン、マリアナ、ヤップ、パラオにおいて軍事支配を確立した。これにより日本は、自国の海岸線防備に不可欠な島々を獲得したのである。それは、アメリカが太平洋岸の防備の枢要であるハワイ、ミッドウェイ、ウェイク、グアムの所有権を主張したのと同様である。ミクロネシアの島々は1914年に、ドイツから日本の手に移管された。それは、ミクロネシアが戦略的に僅少価値しかなかった国から、それを軍事的優位のために利用できる国の手に渡されたということである。

　欧州戦線でのドイツの敗北が確実になると、日本は太平洋の新植民地を合法化しようと行動を起こした。1917年、日本は大英帝国その他僅かな国々と秘密条約を締結して、ミクロネシアの所有権が日本に属するものと国際的に認められることを確かなものとした。そして1922年のベルサイユ会議で、日本は正式にこれらの島々の統治を国際連合から委任され、その統轄、内務の管理が委託された。

　1930年半ばまでにまたしても、地球上には暗雲が立ちこめた。軍事施設の建設は委任の約定により禁じられていたが、日本は熱心に島々の強化を図った。そしてトラックは、当時太平洋で最強、巨大で機動性を備えた日本海軍の進撃基地となるべく準備されていった。

　戦争勃発時、真珠湾を措いて、トラックは太平洋における最強の海軍基地との評価を得ていた。トラックが難攻不落の要塞、「太平洋のジブラルタル」との評価を受けたのは、日本陸・海軍が駐屯していたからというよりも、その自然環境、地形が防衛に適していたことによる。山脈が沈没してできたトラックの11の島は、周囲200キロあまりの珊瑚礁に囲まれている。環礁には5つの水道しかなく、水中機雷や沿岸砲から島を護ることは容易である。米海軍には、環礁外から島の軍事目標まで到達する大砲がないので、水陸攻撃をしようとすればどうしても、環礁内に入り込み、海面下に潜む無数の珊瑚礁に策を弄し、また各島々を縁取っている小環礁を通過できる航路を探し、さらに沿岸砲台からの砲撃を避けなければならない。たとえ日本の軍事技師によって手が加えられ

break inside the outer reef, maneuver around countless submerged coral beds, locate a path through the fringing reefs surrounding each of the islands, and avoid gunfire from Japanese shore batteries. Even without improvements by Japanese military engineers, Truk's natural defenses made it a formidable base and an excellent anchorage for the Imperial Japanese Navy.

On November 15, 1939, the Japanese Fourth Fleet was organized and subsequently ordered to protect the Mandated Islands. Since Truk was located in the center of the Carolines, about 600 miles from Rabaul and 650 miles from the Solomons, it was a natural choice for the headquarters for the Fourth Fleet. Under command of this fleet were the garrisons at Saipan, Kwajalein, Tarawa, and Nauru Island - - all the principal Japanese bases in the Central Pacific.

With the arrival of the Fourth Fleet at Truk, construction began on a seaplane base, naval repair facilities, and administration buildings. The facilities of the naval base were very limited in keeping with Japan's restricted budget. Hence, only relatively minor ship repairs were possible at Truk; major work had to be done in the yards in Japan. A large enemy fleet would find Truk lacking in the proper facilities to keep them operating at full strength.

It was not until the end of 1940 that the first military fortifications were installed in Truk. In November of that year, six guns of 1895 Sino-Japanese vintage were installed for coastal defense on Tol, Moen, and Uman Islands. Eleven three-inch surface guns were mounted on reef islands guarding each of the passes, and six anti-aircraft guns were placed on Dublon, Fefen, and Eten Islands. A defense unit of about 900 men was deployed to operate these guns.

In January 1944, 7500 army troops moved into Truk in preparation for an expected Allied invasion. They started construction of beach defenses and pillboxes and installed six more coast-defense batteries and about eighty more anti-aircraft emplacements. The navy installed rocket launchers and developed torpedo boats and the one-man torpedo to defend the islands. The boats, Daihatsu landing craft armed with one torpedo attached to each side, were kept in rock revetments among mangrove swamps on the edge of Moen and Uman Islands. The one-man controlled torpedo was a standard Model 91 torpedo altered with a streamlined cockpit to hold the operator, who would guide his craft toward an enemy ship. This was not intended to be a suicide weapon as the pilot was expected to leave the torpedo when assured that it would hit its target. The torpedoes were housed in caves cut into rocky hillsides on the larger islands, with tracks laid from the caves over the fringing reefs to the open water.

The Japanese were quick to recognize that Truk was ideal for the mine warfare. They planted more than 2000 submerged contact mines inside the reef at the five passes, and about 6000 beach mines around the larger, interior islands. Anti-submarine nets guarded the Dublon and Uman anchorages.

After Admiral Yamamoto was killed early in 1943, Admiral Koga took command of the combined fleet using the super-battleship *Musashi* as his flagship. The combined fleet stationed at Truk at that time consisted of four battleships, twelve cruis-

なかったとしても、トラックは、その防衛に適した自然環境のお陰で、敵を寄せつけない基地、この上もない好投錨地なのであった。

1939年11月15日、日本の第4艦隊が組織され、続いてそれに、委任統治の島々の防衛が命じられた。トラックは、ラバウルからほぼ1,000キロ、ソロモン群島からも1,000キロ余りのカロリン諸島のほぼ中心に位置しているので、第四艦隊の司令部がここに置かれたのは理の当然であった。そして、太平洋中央の主要な日本軍基地——サイパン、クワジェリン、タワラ、ナウル等——はすべてこの艦隊の指揮下に置かれた。

第4艦隊のトラック到着に伴って、水上飛行機基地、海軍補修施設、司令部の建物などの建設が始められた。海軍基地施設は、日本の予算が限られていたために、非常に限られたものでしかなかった。そのためにトラックでは比較的簡単な船の修理しかできず、大きなものは日本本土でしなければならなかった。トラックには、巨大な艦隊がその力を余すところなく発揮するにはあまりにも限られた施設しかなかったのである。

1940年末になって初めて、トラックに最初の軍事要塞が構築された。同年11月、トル（水曜島）、モエン（春島）、ウマン（冬島）には沿岸防備用に、旧式の大砲6基が据えられた。それぞれの水道守備のためには、3インチ水上砲が11基、珊瑚の島々に設置された。また高射砲6基が、ドゥブロン（夏島）、フェーフェン（秋島）、エテン（竹島）に据えられた。そしてその操作のため、約900人からなる1個守備隊が配された。

1944年1月には、連合軍の侵略に備えるため7,500人の陸軍部隊がトラックにやってきた。そして、沿岸防御施設、防空壕の建設に着手し、さらに6基の沿岸防御要塞を築き、80の高射砲を設置した。海軍の方では、ロケット発射装置を設置し、魚雷艇や一人用魚雷艇を開発した。それはダイハツの上陸用舟艇の両側に1個ずつの魚雷を装備したもので、それらはモエンやウマン外縁のマングローブ樹海の岩間に隠されていた。一人用の魚雷艇は91型魚雷を改造して流線型の操縦席をつけたものである。操縦者は自分で敵船に向って艇を動かすのである。しかしこれは決して、自殺武器と意図されたものではない。操縦者は、魚雷が標的に命中すると確信した時点で、その魚雷から離れるものと思われていたからである。これらの魚雷艇は、大きな島の岩場の洞穴に格納され、その洞穴から海中の裾礁には線路が敷設されていた。

日本軍はトラックが機雷戦に絶好であることを速やかに理解した。そして環礁の5水道付近に2,000以上もの触発機雷をしかけ、また大きな島の周りには6,000もの水雷を設置した。ドゥブロンとウマンの投錨港には対潜水艦用にネットが張られた。

1943年（昭和18年）初め、山本海軍大将亡きあとを継いで、古賀海軍大将が連合艦隊の指揮にあたった。彼は戦艦「武蔵」を旗艦とした。当時トラックに集結していた連合艦隊は、戦艦4隻、巡洋艦12隻、航空母艦4隻、潜水艦12隻、多くの輸送船から成っていた。トラックは海軍基地であったため、航空隊も日本海軍の指揮下におかれていた。飛行場は、エテン（竹島）、パラム（楓島）、モエ

ers, four carriers, twelve submarines, and a large merchant-support fleet. Since Truk was a naval base, its air force was operated and commanded by the Japanese Navy. The airstrips were located on Eten, Param, and Moen Islands, with two seaplane bases, one each on Dublon and Moen Islands. Eten field, by far the best of the airstrips, was used primarily as a fighter base.

For the American high command, Truk was the object of much speculation; almost nothing was known about it. Even Admiral Marc Mitscher, Commander of Task Force 58, admitted that all he knew about Truk was what he read in *National Geographic.* No westerner was believed to have seen the atoll in twenty-five years, since the Japanese had closed the area to virtually all outside contact. Some even believed that Truk was Amelia Earhart's real objective in her attempted around-the-world flight in 1937, and they speculated that she was trying to photograph the Japanese base with secret cameras when she was shot down and captured.

What strategy should US naval planners use against Truk? After the bloody capture of Tarawa in November 1943, the Joint Chiefs of Staff had second thoughts about the wisdom of launching direct amphibious assaults against heavily fortified islands. US ground forces paid a heavy price at Tarawa; 1075 killed and 2353 wounded. Marine Commander Holland Smith, convinced that the invasion was a "terrible waste of life and effort", argued that Tarawa should have been neutralized by air strikes, cut off from supply lines, and then bypassed altogether. It was clear that a new tactic was needed for the impending strike on Truk.

In January 1944, the Joint Chiefs of Staff decided in favor of a swift, two-day air strike--code-named Operation Hailstone--led from three task groups. From Eniwetok in the Marshalls Islands, Admiral Raymond Spruance ordered six battleships, ten cruisers, nine aircraft carriers, and thirty escorting destroyers southwest to Truk atoll in what would become the biggest battle until then in the Pacific war. This attack on Truk marked the evolution of American strategy in the Pacific: the destruction of a major enemy base without the aid of landbased air-power and without any follow-up by amphibious forces. Beginning with the Truk raid, this method of neutralizing forces was followed until the Japanese surrender in 1945.

At 6:30 AM on February 16, 1944, seventy-two F6F Hellcat fighters, led by Commander William Kane and launched from the decks of the carriers *Enterprise, Yorktown, Essex, Intrepid,* and *Bunker Hill,* climbed into the morning sky. Ninety miles northeast of Truk Lagoon the powerful snub-nosed fighters were roaring through the dawn in three groups of twenty-four at an altitude of ten, fifteen, and twenty thousand feet. Their mission was to clear the skies of enemy planes over the lagoon so that Dauntless dive-bombers and Avenger torpedo-bombers could knock out Japanese shipping and military installations.

As the blue fighters came in over the reef, forty to fifty Japanese fighters--Zekes, Hamps, Rufes, and Tojos--were taking off and climbing rapidly to meet them. The attacking carrier planes had been picked up by radar almost thirty minutes before their arrival over the lagoon, but most islands only had ten minutes advance warning because of a lack of an effective communication system. Most of the trained fighter

ン（春島）にあり、また水上飛行機の基地は、ドゥブロンとモエンにあった。エテンの飛行場は決して最上のものではなかったが、主に戦闘機基地として使用された。

米軍司令部にとって、トラックはいろいろな思惑が生じるところであった。というのは、トラックについてはほとんど何も知られていなかったからである。第58機動部隊の司令官、マーク・ミッチェル海将でさえ、トラックについては『ナショナル・ジオグラフィック』誌の記事を読んだだけで、それ以外何も知らないと述べている。日本がその地域で実質的に外部との交渉を絶って25年このかた、西海岸の人間でも、トラックを見た者はひとりもいないと思われていた。また、1937年にアメリア・エアハルトが世界一周飛行を企てたのはトラックを見るためであり、彼女はトラックの日本軍基地を撮影しようとして、撃ち落とされ捕えられたのだというような話が、一部の人には信じられるほどだった。

米海軍作戦本部は、トラックに対していかなる戦略をとるべきか。1943年11月、タラワでは悽惨な捕獲にあったので、その後統合参謀本部は、堅牢強固な島々に陸海共同の直接攻撃を開始するのは賢明かどうか再考した。米軍地上部隊はタラワにおいて、死者1,075人、負傷者2,353人と高い代価を払った。海軍司令官ホランド・スミスは、水平侵略は生命と努力の著しい浪費であると確信し、タラワにおいては、空からの攻撃によって敵の戦力を弱め、補給路を断ち、その後で陸海共同で敵を攻めるべきであったのだと論じた。とにかくさし迫ったトラック攻撃に新しい作戦が必要なことは明らかであった。

1944年1月、統合参謀本部は、3つの機動部隊による迅速な、2日間の空からの攻撃——霰作戦——を行なうことで合意した。レイモンド・スプルアンス海将の命令を受けて、戦艦6隻、巡洋艦10隻、航空母艦9隻、護衛駆逐艦30隻が、マーシャル群島のエニウェトクから南西に向い、トラック環礁近くに結集した。そこで太平洋戦史上、それまでで最大の激戦が展開することになるのである。このトラック攻撃は、太平洋における米軍の戦略に進展をもたらした。つまり、陸上航空隊を恃まず、水陸両軍の攻撃に依らずして、敵の主要基地を破壊したのである。このトラック空襲を緒として1945年に日本が降伏するまで、敵戦力を無力化するためにこの方法がとられ続けた。

1944年2月16日午前6時半、F6F「じゃじゃ馬」戦闘機72機が、司令官ウィリアム・ケインに指揮されて、空母「エンタープライズ」、「ヨークタウン」、「エセックス」、「イントレピッド」、「バンカーヒル」の甲板から暁の空に飛び立った。鷲鼻の戦闘機は、トラック北西150キロの空に力強く爆音を響かせた。72機は24機ずつ3編成をとり、それぞれ高度3,000、4,500、6,000メートルを飛んだ。その使命は、急降下爆撃機や雷撃機が、日本の輸送設備、軍事施設を爆撃できるように、環礁上空の敵機を一掃することであった。

青い戦闘機が環礁上空に来ると、日本の戦闘機——陸軍の零戦、海軍の零戦、零式水上機、鍾馗——4〜50機が、離陸し迎え撃ってきた。米軍の攻撃用艦上機は環礁上空到達約30分前にレーダーに捕えられていたが、効果的な通信網の不備のため、ほとんどの島では10分前になってやっと警報が出される始末だっ

pilots were quartered on Dublon Island, far from their aircraft on Eten and Moen Islands.

For the next hour the American pilots engaged in the most vicious air battle they had ever experienced. During the first twenty minutes of battle, a burning plane fell through the sky every thirty seconds. Fighter after fighter zoomed and dived in a tangled array of screaming machinery. The airfields were cluttered with taxiing Japanese fighters trying to join the battle and the sky overhead was filling with smoke from blazing aircraft. Tracers of anti-aircraft fire streaked up at the carrier planes. The scene over the once placid Truk Lagoon had become a garish nightmare.

As they approached Dublon Island, "Killer" Kane and his wingman met a squadron of Zekes and quickly ripped two of them apart. Moments later, they caught two more Japanese planes trying to take off from Eten Island's fighter base. As they rose from their strafing run, another Zeke made a sloppy attempt to intercept them, but they easily destroyed the orange and black fighter. Kane and his wingman scored five planes in the first five minutes of action.

Lieutenant "Frenchy" Reulet tailed a Zeke through a loop and managed to burn him before his Hellcat stalled out. He then followed a "Rufe" floatplane into a dive, let loose a volley of machinegun fire and watched the thin-skinned enemy aircraft disintegrate. Minutes later, scoring another kill on a Hamp, he saw the pilot's clothes ignite as he bailed out of the burning plane. Swinging gently below the blossomed parachute was a human fireball. As Reulet's eyes were glued to this grisly scene he failed to notice a Rufe floatplane closing in on his tail, but his alert wingman quickly destroyed the Japanese fighter.

Ensign "Flash" Gordon, who found himself alone in a head-on approach with four Zekes, shot down two of them before diving away with his guns jammed. Lieutenant Jack Farley shot down a Rufe from behind in a sharp turn, but a twenty millimeter shell exploded in his cockpit, shattering his instrument panel and lacerating his hands and legs. Farley's plane still flew, so he dived and strafed Param Island's airfield, catching a Zeke trying to take off. As the Zeke splashed into the harbor, Farley swung away from the action and nursed his Hellcat back to his ship.

By 9:30 AM the Hellcats were in control of the skies over Truk Lagoon. More than thirty enemy fighters had been shot down and forty more were destroyed on the ground. Only four Hellcats were missing.

Thirty more strikes, each made up of eighteen to thirty Dauntless dive-bombers, Avenger torpedo-bombers, and escorting Hellcats, were launched from the carriers. Their mission was to destroy enemy shipping and the three airfields in Truk. Loaded with fragmentation clusters and incendiaries, the bombers managed to sink all Japanese naval vessels and twenty merchant ships. Each of the thirty attacks was stronger than either of the two attacks made by the Japanese at Pearl Harbor. The airfields on Eten, Moen, and Param Islands were pockmarked with deep craters, preventing any Japanese aircraft from taking off and intercepting the Americans.

In the hours before dawn on February 17, the first carrier based night bombing

た。その上、熟練した戦闘機のパイロットたちは、飛行場のあるモエン、エテンから遥か離れたドゥブロンに宿営していたのである。

　１時間の空中戦で、米軍パイロットたちはかつてなかったほどの勝利を収めた。最初の20分間、ほぼ毎分ごとに敵機が炎上し墜落していった。飛行場は戦闘に飛び立とうとしている飛行機でごった返し、上空は炎上する飛行機の煙がもうもうとしていた。また高射砲から戦闘機目がけて発射される曳光弾が筋を画いていた。かつて静穏であったトラック環礁の上空にも、けばけばしい悪夢が画かれたのである。

　ドゥブロンに接近すると、「殺し屋」ケインとその部下は零戦の一隊に出くわしたが、それを撃破し、続いてエテン飛行場から離陸しようとしていた戦闘機２機をもやっつけた。機銃掃射の体勢を整えようと上昇すると、別の零戦がそれを迹ぎろうとしたが、そのオレンジと黒の戦闘機をも容易に撃墜した。ケインとその部下たちは初めの５分間の行動で、敵機５機を撃破した。

　「フランス野郎」ルーレイ中尉は筋斗返りで零戦の後につき、自分の戦闘機が失速しないうちに敵機を撃ち落とした。続いて急降下する零式水上機を追い機銃掃射を浴びせ、薄い機体の敵機を撃破した。数分後には、海軍零戦を撃ち、炎上する機体から脱出しようとする飛行士の服に火がついているのを目撃した。ゆっくりと揺れ落ちる落下傘は火の玉と化していた。ルーレイがこの凄じい光景に見とれている間に、別の零式水上機が背後に迫っていたが、味方の機に助けられて危うく難を逃れた。

　「稲妻」ゴードン少尉は上空から４機の零戦に迫られた時自分ひとりであったが、そのうちの２機を撃墜し、急降下してその場を逃れた。ジャック・ファーレイ中尉は、急旋回して後についていた零式水上機を撃墜したが、操縦席で20ミリ弾が破裂し、計器制御盤が壊れ、自らも手足に裂傷を負った。ファーレイの機はなおも飛び続け、パラム飛行場目がけて降下し、機銃掃射をかけ、離陸しようとしていた零戦を１機しとめた。零戦が港に飛び込むのを見てファーレイは行動を止め、愛機をいたわりながら母艦に戻った。

　午前９時半までに「じゃじゃ馬」はトラック環礁の上空を制した。敵戦闘機は30機あまりが撃墜され、40余機が地上で破壊された。一方「じゃじゃ馬」戦闘機のほうは、４機がやられたのみだった。

　急降下爆撃機、雷撃機、護衛戦闘機、18～30機が編隊を組み空母を発進し、30回にわたって爆撃が行なわれた。その使命は、トラックの敵船舶、３つの飛行場を破壊することであった。破砕弾、焼夷弾を積載した爆撃機は日本海軍の全艦と商船20隻を沈没させた。この１回の爆撃は、日本軍が真珠湾で行なった２度の爆撃のいずれよりも強力であった。エテン、モエン、パラムの飛行場は深い砲弾穴であばたのようになり、ために日本軍機は離陸できず、米軍機を阻止することができなかった。

　２月17日未明、空母を拠点とする夜襲が初めて行なわれ、「エンタープライズ」の甲板から爆撃機が発進していった。ＴＢＦ雷撃機「復讐者」には、レーダー、500ポンド爆弾４つが搭載されていた。またその爆弾には、低空飛行をしても

空襲下夏島沖の日本船舶、1944年2月16日

Japanese fleet under attack off Dublon Island, February 16, 1944 (National Archives Photo)

Torpedo hits *Amagisan Maru*, off Uman Island
(National Archives Photos)

冬島近くの天城山丸に魚雷命中

'Hellcat' strafes beached Japanese destroyer

日本の駆逐艦への機銃掃射

attack of the war was launched from the deck of the *Enterprise.* Twelve TBF Avenger torpedo-bombers were equipped with radar and four 500-pound bombs with time delay fuses to allow the low-flying aircraft to escape the blast of their own bombs. At 3:40 AM the Avengers began the attack. Sweeping into the lagoon at 180 knots, they picked out the largest ships and bore in on them at an altitude of 250 feet. Just as the dark mass of the target disappeared under the nose of the Avenger, the radarman yelled "Mark" and the pilot released his bombs. The four-second delay fuses gave the pilot just enough time to clear the explosion and bank around for another run. Ship after ship was attacked in this fashion, and soon the night sky was glowing with flames from sinking vessels. Anti-aircraft fire was intense but inaccurate as the invisible attackers skimmed over the crowded anchorage.

After the last run, the Avengers closed their bomb-bay doors and rendezvoused southwest of the atoll. They left behind a lagoon full of burning, sinking ships; two tankers and six freighters were already on their way to the bottom. This raid proved the feasibility of night, low-altitude radar bombing. Half the runs made by the aircraft scored hits, while only about one-fifth of the daylight attacks were successful. The experiment showed that these night attacks were several times more accurate than daytime missions, during which a fighter escort was necessary and anti-aircraft fire was much more effective.

During the daylight hours of February 17, the American forces launched three final strikes. Not a single enemy fighter was in the air as Dauntless dive-bombers, Avengers, and Hellcats strafed and bombed the airfields and any remaining shipping. The second strike concentrated on the fuel supply depot of Dublon Island--a target Mitscher's pilots had been saving for the last attack. Over 10,000 pounds of bombs were dropped by the SBD's, and a cloud of oily smoke rose 8,000 feet over the target. Truk was destroyed as a major base.

The strike on Truk was one of the most successful naval operations of the war. More than 490 tons of bombs and torpedoes had been dropped on shipping, airfields, and shore installations. The light cruisers *Naka, Agano,* and *Katori,* seaplane tender *Akitsushima,* auxilliary cruisers *Aikoku Maru* and *Kiyosumi Maru,* destroyers *Fumizuki, Yubure, Oikaze* and *Nagatsuki,* aircraft ferry *Fujikawa Maru,* sub-tenders *Rio de Janeiro Maru* and *Heian Maru,* six tankers, and about twenty other vessels were sunk---in all about forty ships totalling 200,000 tons. The strike on Truk reduced the supply capability of the base by seventy-five percent and destroyed 265 Japanese planes. American losses were extraordinarily light; twenty-five planes were downed and forty men were killed in action. Truk's usefulness as a fleet anchorage and advanced naval base was ended.

Crippled as it was by the February strike, Truk was battered a second time on April 29, 1944. In the two and one-half months since the American fleet had last engaged Truk, Japan had abandoned their base as a fleet anchorage. Most of the shipping had left the atoll, but it was reinforced with more anti-aircraft positions, fighters, bombers, and patrol aircraft, and its garrison of army troops was increased to 14,300 men. The objective in this sweep was the destruction of all ground installations, buildings, aircraft, and any remaining shipping.

爆弾の炸裂から自機を守ることができるよう時限信管が取りつけられていた。午前5時40分、「復讐者」の攻撃が開始された。時速320キロでトラック上空に襲来し、大型船舶に目標を定め、高度約76メートルから爆撃した。標的が「復讐者」の鼻先に隠れるとレーダー操者が「目標」と叫び、飛行士が爆弾を投下するのである。爆弾は4秒後に炸裂するようになっているので、この間にパイロットは爆風から逃れ、次の爆撃体制を整える。このようにして船は次々に爆撃を受け、未だ明けやらぬ空は、沈みゆく船の炎で赤く染められた。高射砲からはひっきりなしに発砲されたが、不正確極まりなく、まるで透明攻撃者が、混雑した停泊地をかすめ過ぎていくようであった。

　最後の爆撃を終え、「復讐者」は弾倉の戸を閉じ、トラック環礁の南西部に集結した。その後には、島のあちこちから火の手が上がり、多くの船舶の沈み行く光景が残された。2隻のタンカーと6隻の貨物船は、すでに海底近くまで沈んでいっていた。この空襲によって夜間の低空飛行でレーダーを利用する爆撃の実効性が明らかにされた。昼間の攻撃では確率5分の1だったものが、今回投下された爆弾の半分は命中したのである。今回の試みによって夜襲が昼間の作戦より数倍確実であることがわかった。昼間だと護衛の戦闘機が必要であり、また高射砲でやられる可能性も大であったのである。

　2月17日の昼間、米軍は3度にわたる爆撃を行なった。急降下爆撃機「不屈者」、「復讐者」雷爆機、そして「じゃじゃ馬」戦闘機が飛行場と残りの船舶に機銃掃射を浴びせ、爆弾を投下した時には、空に敵戦闘機は1機もなかった。2回目の爆撃では、ドゥブロンの給油施設に照準があてられた。それは前回の爆撃でミッチェル隊が残しておいたものだった。総計1万ポンドを上回る爆弾がSBDから投下され、地上からは油煙がもくもく上がり、2,500メートル上空にまで達した。トラックは主要基地であったので、徹底的に破壊されたのである。

　トラック爆撃は、米海軍の作戦のうちで最も成功したものだった。爆弾、魚雷が総計490トン以上も、船舶、飛行場、沿岸施設に投下された。そして、軽巡洋艦「なか」「あがの」「かとり」、水上機護衛艦「あきつしま」、補助巡洋艦「愛国丸」「清澄丸」、駆逐艦「ふみつき」「ゆうぐれ」「おいかぜ」「ながつき」、飛行機運搬船「富士川丸」、潜水艦母艦「りおで志"やねろ丸」「平安丸」、タンカー6隻、その他20余隻、合計50隻20万トンにものぼる船舶が沈没させられた。これに比して米軍の損失は極めて少なかった。撃墜された航空機が25機、戦死者が40名であった。トラックの、艦隊の停泊地、海軍の前進基地としての有用性も、これをもって終りを告げた。

　2月の爆撃でトラックを半死半生にした米軍は、1944年4月29日に再度攻撃をかけた。前回の戦闘から2ヶ月半の間に、日本軍は艦隊の停泊地トラックを見離した。ほとんどの船舶がトラックを離れ、それに代って、高射砲、戦闘機、爆撃機、哨戒機が増やされ、陸軍の防備隊も1万4,300人に増員されていた。今回の攻撃の目的は、地上施設、建物、航空機、そして残りの船舶をことごとく破壊することであった。

空襲下夏島沖の船舶、1944年4月29日

Shipping near Dublon Island under attack, April 29 1944 (National Archives Photos)

Jubilant U.S. fighter pilots aboard *USS Langley*
(National Archives Photos).

トラック空襲後、USSラングリー船上で、
歓喜する戦闘隊員

Dublon Island after U.S. attack, April 30, 1944.

米軍空襲後の夏島、1944年4月30日

The Japanese had a half hour's advance warning of the approaching Hellcats and they were able to send up fifty-seven intercepting aircraft at the first assault wave of eighty-four planes. Anti-aircraft fire was heavy and accurate, even though there was a thick cloud layer at 5,000 feet. Still, the Japanese fighters seemed reluctant to engage the Americans, perhaps remembering their losses in the first raid.

In one of the most aggressive battles that day, Lieutenant Robert Kanze attacked a Zeke head-on. As the two pilots furiously flew straight towards each other with all guns firing, both planes caught fire and the pilots bailed out. Kanze plopped safely into the lagoon, inflated his rubber raft and paddled towards the South Pass, where he hoped he would be picked up by a patroling submarine or floatplane assigned to rescue downed pilots. The next day a floatplane spotted Kanze and landed in the choppy sea. When the small "Kingfisher" reached Kanze, he grabbed the small wing float but suddenly his raft shot out from under him and the force of his weight on the port wing capsized the Kingfisher, dumping its two crewmen into the sea.

Later, another Kingfisher, flown by Lieutenant John Burns, landed and the three men carefully climbed to balanced positions; one on each wing and one on the large float below the fuselage. The pilot then taxied to the surfaced submarine *Tang* and put his passengers aboard. Burns took off again from the choppy sea and soon found another downed pilot east of Truk. Burns landed and picked up the pilot, but after three attempts he could not get his plane airborne. The combination of rough water and extra weight was too much for the little Kingfisher, so he radioed for help. Three hours later the submarine *Tang* surfaced again and headed for the floatplane. Meanwhile, Burns had picked up six more downed airmen as he taxied around the Pacific in a scout plane that could not fly. At last he met the *Tang* and put his crewman and passengers aboard. Damaged beyond repair, the battered plane was sunk by machinegunners on the submarine. Crowded with twenty-two airmen she had picked up during the two-day strike, including the six pilots Burns rescued, the *Tang* rejoined the US fleet.

By the end of this raid the Americans had shot down sixty-three Japanese aircraft and destroyed sixty more on the ground. A total of 748 tons of bombs were dropped, demolishing 423 buildings and damaging forty-five others. Shipping losses included the *Dai na Hino*, the *Sapporo Maru*, the *Minsei Maru*, and at least twenty other vessels. Twenty-two American aircraft were lost in this second carrier attack and nineteen airmen were killed. This casualty list could have been much higher but of the forty-six downed airmen, twenty-eight were rescued by the *Tang* and other submarines.

During the entire campaign against Truk more than 416 Japanese aircraft were destroyed. Naval and merchant shipping losses totaled over sixty vessels sunk inside and outside the lagoon. Airfields that had been repaired after the first American carrier attack were again severely damaged and island installations were eighty percent destroyed. The few Japanese planes left intact were sent to Yap and Guam, leaving Truk defenseless from any further air attacks. Only seven aircraft were op-

日本軍は「じゃじゃ馬」戦闘機の襲来に対し半時間前に警報を発令し、84機による第一波の攻撃には、57機の要撃戦闘機を繰り出した。上空1,500メートルは厚い雲に被われていたが、高射砲の攻撃は激しく、しかも正確であった。しかしながら米軍に立ち向う日本軍戦闘機は、前回の空襲での敗北が頭に残っているせいであろうか、心なしか怖気ているようであった。

　その日の激戦において、ロバート・カンズ少尉は零戦と正面から撃ち合った。「じゃじゃ馬」「零戦」の両機ともに機銃掃射をしながら直進し、両機は火を吹き、飛行士は落下傘で脱出した。カンズ少尉は、海面に無事に着くとゴム筏をふくらませ、南水道に向けて漕ぎ出した。そうすれば、不時着した飛行士を救助するための巡回潜水艦か水上飛行機に助け上げられるだろうと期待していた。翌日になって、水上機がカンズを発見し、波高い海に着水した。小型水上機「カワセミ」がそばに来ると、カンズはその小さな翼浮子につかまった。がその途端、筏が下から撃ち抜かれた。彼の体の重みが左翼にどっとかかったので「カワセミ」は転覆し、2人の乗組員も海に拠げ出された。

　しばらくしてジョン・バーンズ少尉の乗った別の「カワセミ」が到着したので、3人はバランスを取りながら機に這い上がった。1人が左翼から、1人が右翼から、そして別の1人は胴体の下の大きな浮子の上に上がった。そして機は海面を滑走して浮上中の潜水艦「タング」に向い、そこで3人をおろした。バーンズ少尉は再び高波から飛び立ち、トラック東方に1人の飛行士が漂流しているのを見つけた。バーンズ少尉は機を着水させ、飛行士を救助した。そして飛び立とうとしたが機は浮上せず、3度試みてみたがだめだった。時化のためと余分な重みが加わったために、小さな「カワセミ」にはどうしようもなかった。そこで無線で救援を求めた。3時間後に潜水艦「タング」が浮上し、水上機に向かってきた。この間にバーンズ少尉は浮上できない偵察機で近辺を滑走し、漂流中の飛行士6人を救助した。やがて「タング」が到着し、水上機に乗っていた者は全員潜水艦に移った。水上機は修理不可能なほどに損傷を受けていたので、潜水艦の機銃で海に沈めた。「タング」は2日間の爆撃中に、バーンズ少尉が救助した6人を含めて合計22人を救助し、米軍艦隊に合流した。

　この空襲の終りまでに米軍は、日本軍の飛行機を63機撃墜し、地上でも60機以上を破壊した。総計748トンの爆弾を投下し、423の建物を崩潰し、44の建物に損害を与えた。船舶の損失には、「第二日野丸」「札幌丸」「民生丸」その他少なくとも20の船が数えられる。一方米軍の方は、今第二回目の航空母艦からの攻撃で、航空機22機を失ない、19人の飛行士が戦死した。この死傷者名簿にはもっと多くの名が記されたかも知れないが、撃墜された飛行士46人中、28人もが「タング」や他の潜水艦に救助されたのである。

　全トラック戦役を通じて、日本軍の飛行機は416機以上が破壊され、軍艦・商船は総計50隻あまりが失なわれた。それらは環礁内外に沈んだのである。第一回目の空襲後に補修された飛行場は再び甚大な被害を受け、島の施設も80パーセントが崩壊した。無傷で残った少数の飛行機はヤップとグアムに移され、トラックはほとんど無防備の状態で残された。1944年6月から終戦に至るまで、

トラックの降服

The surrender of Truk (National Archives Photo)

トラックには7機の飛行機しかなかった。3つの主要飛行場は4月30日の爆撃後は見捨てられたままだった。こうしてトラックは孤立状態に残されてしまった。

　終結は速やかにやってきた。1945年8月15日、日本は無条件降服を宣言した。トラック駐屯軍司令官、原忠一海軍中将はトラックからグアムに無電を打ち、交渉を始めたい意向を示唆した。これを受けてグアムに合衆国海軍使節団が組織され、予備会談が直ちに行なわれるべきであるとの伝言をトラックに送った。日本軍司令官は、8月30日に南水道近くで合衆国側と会見することに合意した。駆逐艦「スタッフ」と駆逐護衛艦「オズムス」はグアムを後に、トラック環礁の南に向かった。そこで日本側使節団を待っている間に、B-24爆撃機6機も到着し、上空を旋回した。白旗を掲げた小型船が南水道から姿をみせ、アメリカ側の船に近づいてきた。そして澄川海軍大将に率いられた5人の退役将校が「スタッフ」に乗船した。

　会談は日本が統治していたギルバート、マーシャル、マリアナ、カロリン諸島——900万平方キロメートルに及ぶ区域にある全島の放棄に関して始められた。トラックの条件については、特にその守備兵力が2万4,000人にも及ぶ陸海軍になっていたために、徹底的に話し合われた。日本側が提出した精密海図によって、環礁内外に精巧にしかけられた機雷敷設面、主な島々の周りに設けられた沿岸防備物が明らかにされた。沿岸防備砲と高射砲は、5水道、外環礁とその中の島々を悉く守備範囲にしていた。弾薬も30日間の激戦に間に合うほどあった。

　陸海軍の防備施設は大がかりでしかも良く整備されていたが、空軍力はわずかで、使用可能な飛行機は全部で7機しかなかった。飛行場は前回の爆撃で全く荒廃してしまい、わずかに小型飛行機が利用できるだけだった。日本海軍には今や、一握りの小型艦載艇、曳航船、港湾航行船などが残っているだけだった。大型船舶は全部沈没し、ラグーン内はおろかトラック周辺には1隻の姿もなかった。ラグーン内には難破船が散在していたので、航行は極めて危険であった。

　トラックはひどい食糧不足に見舞われていた。帝国海軍が本土に引き上げてからは供給が中断されたので、全住民には畑を耕したり魚を獲ることが強制された。島の日本人は、さつま芋と野菜、そして時々魚を食べて命をつないでいた。戦争の最後の年には、アメリカ軍の戦線をくぐり抜けてトラックに幾許かでも食糧や医薬品を補給できたのは、わずかに7隻の輸送潜水艦だけであった。島の日本病院には、栄養失調の患者が溢れていた。

　暑い夏の昼下り、降服についての交渉が進むにつれて、日本側と米国側にあった緊張は次第に消散していった。澄川海軍大将以下日本軍使節は長時間にわたる会談で、子細に至るまで丁重で礼儀に適っていた。日本側には、すべての武器、戦闘具を集め、沿岸砲、高射砲をすべて撤廃する、ラグーン内、水道付近にしかけられた機雷はすべて除去する、飛行機の離着陸が可能なようできるだけ飛行場を修復することが指示された。日本側は、連合軍に対するいかなる

erational on Truk from June 1944 until the end of the war. The three major airfields were abandoned after the April 30 raid. Truk was left to stand alone.

The end was quick in coming; on August 15, 1945, the Japanese announced their unconditional surrender. A radio dispatch from Truk to Guam authorized by Vice Admiral Chuichi Hara, commander of the Truk garrison, indicated his willingness to begin negotiations. A US naval mission was organized on Guam and a message was sent to Truk stating that preliminary discussions should be held immediately. The Japanese commander agreed to meet the US team on August 30, just outside the South Pass. The destroyer *Stack* and the destroyer escort *Ozmus* left Guam and rendezvoused south of the atoll. Six B-24 bombers arrived overhead to fly cover for the ships as they waited for the Japanese mission. A small boat showing a white flag appeared out of the pass, headed toward the American ships, and discharged five Japanese officers, led by Admiral Sumigawa, aboard the *Stack.*

Discussions were begun on the surrender of all Japanese-held islands in the Gilberts, Marshalls, Marianas, and Carolines--an area of three and a half million square miles. Conditions in Truk were thoroughly discussed, especially since garrison strength had grown to 24,000 army and navy troops. Detailed charts brought out by the Japanese revealed elaborate patterns of mine fields both inside and outside the lagoon and beach defenses surrounding all major islands. Coastal defense batteries and anti-aircraft emplacements covered the five passes, the reef, and the islands within the reef, and there was enough ammunition for thirty days of hard fighting.

Although the naval and army defense facilities were large and well equipped, the air-force was limited to a total of seven operational aircraft. Airfields were in such poor condition from previous bombing that only light model fighters were capable of using them. The Japanese Navy consisted of a handful of small barges, tugs, and harbor craft; not a single large vessel remained unsunk in the lagoon or even in the vicinity of the atoll. The lagoon anchorage was littered with so many wrecks that navigation was extremely hazardous.

Truk was desperately short of food. The entire population was forced to cultivate gardens and fish since Truk was cut off from supplies after the retreat of the Imperial Navy to home waters. The Japanese were subsisting on sweet potatoes, green vegetables, and occasionally fish. During the last year of the war only seven transport submarines were able to break through American lines to supply Truk with some food and medicine, Japanese hospitals were filled to overflowing with severe cases of malnutrition.

As the surrender negotiations continued through the hot afternoon, tension between the Japanese and American missions slowly dissipated. The Japanese mission under Admiral Sumigawa was cordial and correct in every detail during the long discussions. The Japanese were instructed to assemble all small arms and all other combat equipment, and all coastal guns and anti-aircraft batteries were to be disarmed. Minefields around the passes and inside the lagoon anchorage were to be cleared, and the airfields repaired as well as possible to receive aircraft. The Jap-

軍事行動をも中止することに同意し、また米軍が関心をもっていた軍事品に関する機密を保存すると約束した。トラックの司令官がアメリカ側に協力的で完全な言質を与えても、公式の降服は、帝国政府が正式に日本本土を降服するのを待たねばならなかった。残されたのは、トラックの降服文書に署名することだけであった。

　会議が終ると、日本側はほっとした様子で、アメリカ側の丁重な取り扱いに礼を述べた。そして士官室を整然と退出し、船に戻った。駆逐艦の乗組員は全員で彼らを暖かく見送った。日本側が去ると、アメリカ側の使節もすぐ水陸両用機に乗り込み、日本軍が持ってきた文書を携えてグアムに帰った。

　1945年9月2日、巡洋艦「USSポートランド」は、トラックラグーン内で「USSスタッフ」、「USSオズムス」に合流した。「ポートランド」船上で、ジョージ・マーレイ海軍中将が、陸軍司令官麦倉俊三郎中将、第4艦隊司令長官原忠一中将、南洋庁東支庁長藍原有孝から、トラックの降服文書を受理した。それは太平洋で最大の降服であった。トラックには、軍人民間人を合わせて3万8,000人の日本人がいたのである。

　難攻不落の砦トラックの神話は崩れ去った。2月と4月の第58機動部隊による空母からの爆撃で日本の防衛線の要所が破られ、北太平洋における30年間の日本軍支配が幕を閉じた。「太平洋のジブラルタル」は陥落した。

anese agreed to stop all military action against allied forces and they promised to preserve any equipment of interest to military intelligence. Although the commander of Truk was committed to complete cooperation with the Americans, official surrender could not take place until the Imperial Government had formally surrendered the home islands of Japan. All that remained was the signature of the surrender papers for Truk.

As the conference came to an end, the Japanese appeared cheerful and they thanked the Americans for their courteous treatment. They filed out of the wardroom and climbed down to their boat, under the scrutiny of almost the entire crew of the destroyer. As soon as the Japanese departed, the American mission boarded amphibious aircraft and flew on to Guam with the documents the Japanese brought out to the ship.

On September 2, 1945, the cruiser *USS Portland* rendezvoused with the *USS Stack* and *USS Ozmus* inside Truk Lagoon. Aboard the *Portland,* Vice Admiral George Murray received the surrender of Truk from Lieutenant General Shunzaburo Mugikura, Commander of the Army, Vice Admiral Chuichi Hara, Commander-in-Chief of the Fourth Fleet, and Mr. Aritake Aihara, head of the East Branch South Seas Government. It was the largest surrender in the Pacific; Japanese military and civilian workers on Truk totalled 38,000.

The myth of Truk the impregnable fortress was shattered. The February and April carrier strikes by Task Force 58 had destroyed a key position in Japan's outer defense perimeter and ended thirty years of Japanese military domination in the North Pacific. The "Gilbralter of the Pacific" had fallen.

Bibliography

The Big "E", Commander Edward P. Stafford USN, Ballentine, 1962.

Field Survey of Truk, Duane Denfield, January 1980, Prepared for Historic Preservation Office, Trust Territory of the Pacific.

Handbook of Japanese Military Forces, War Department Technical Manual TME 30-480, October 1, 1944.

History of US Naval Operations in WWII, Volume VII, Aleutians, Gilberts, and Marshalls, June 1942-April 1944, By Samuel Eliot Morison, Little, Brown, and Co., 1951.

History of US Naval Operations in WWII, Volume VIII, New Guinea and the Marianas, March 1944-August 1944, by Samuel Eliot Morison, Little, Brown, and Co., 1951.

The Imperial Japanese Navy, Paul S. Dull, Naval Institute Press, 1978.

Reduction of Truk, US Strategic Bombing Survey, Naval Analysis Division, February 1947.

Silent Victory, Clay Blair Jr., Lippincott, 1975.

The Surrender of the Fortress of Truk, Charles Stuart Blackton, The Pacific Historical Review, Volume XV, December 1946.

US Naval Institute Prodeedings, October 1948, "Truk-South Seas Mystery Base", by Bertram Vogel.

US Naval Institute Proceedings, March 1977, "Hellcats over Truk", by Barett Tillman.